WILMINGTON CHRISTIAN ACADEMY

Amy Carmichael

Can brown eyes be made blue?

The true story of Amy Carmichael
and her looking glass

Catherine Mackenzie
Illustrated by Rita Ammassari

Amy Carmichael lived in a big, tall house by the ocean, with her father, her mother, her brother Norman and her little brother, Ernest. Amy and her brothers would often get into mischief together. Amy liked to think up new and exciting games to play, but what Amy really longed for was an adventure.

Amy lived in a big, tall
house by the ocean.

One day Amy wanted to sail out to sea. It would be so exciting, she thought.

'Come on!' she yelled at her mischievous brothers. 'Let's find a rowing boat!'

When they arrived at the beach they were hot and out of breath. It didn't take them long before they found a little boat tied up on the sands. Soon they were off.

'Hurray, hurray!' Amy squealed. 'We're going on a real adventure now.'

'Let's find a rowing boat!' yelled Amy.

They enjoyed it at first. It was very exciting indeed. But when they got tired they wanted to go home. The strong winds and the choppy waves meant that they couldn't turn the boat around. They kept sailing further, and further out to sea. What were they going to do?

Amy had an idea. 'Let's sing as loudly as we can,' she said.

They kept sailing further
and further out to sea.

A sailor on the shore heard her and came to the rescue.

Amy's mother gave them a telling off when they got home. 'Sailing out to sea is highly dangerous!' she exclaimed. Amy decided not to play that game anymore.

Amy's mother gave them a
telling off when they got home.

One day Amy and her brothers climbed onto the house roof. It would be a great place to see the ocean, Amy thought. And it was. But they got stuck. When Amy's father saw them he got the fright of his life. He ran upstairs and pulled his children back through the bathroom window. Amy's father told her that climbing roofs was 'highly dangerous'. Amy decided not to play that game anymore.

Amy and her brothers climbed
onto the house roof.

Another day Amy was told that eating plum stones would make her ill.

'I wonder if that's really true?' thought Amy.

So Amy sat down and ate twelve plum stones, one after the other. Amy felt very, very sick. Her parents told her that eating plum stones was 'highly dangerous and terribly silly'. Amy decided not to play that game anymore.

Amy sat down and ate twelve
plum stones, one after the other.

One morning Amy lifted up her looking glass. She saw her long dark hair and her soft brown eyes, but her face was sad. 'Brown eyes are boring,' Amy grumbled. She went downstairs and watched her mother make the breakfast.

'Why did God give me brown eyes and not blue?' Amy wondered. 'I'd look pretty if I had blue eyes,' Amy sighed.

'What a strange thing to say,' laughed her mother. 'I think your eyes are beautiful Amy.'

'Brown eyes are boring,' Amy grumbled.

Afterwards when her mother was clearing away the dishes, Amy asked, 'God answers prayers. Doesn't he?'

'Yes Amy, he does,' replied her mother.

'He will answer my prayers. Won't he?' Amy asked.

'Yes, Amy, he will,' her mother smiled.

'He will answer my prayers tonight!' Amy jumped for joy, as she ran into the garden.

Amy's mother looked puzzled. 'What is Amy up to now?' she wondered.

Amy jumped for joy,
as she ran into the garden.

That night Amy prayed to God. 'Please give me blue eyes.' But the next morning they were still brown. 'Why hasn't God answered my prayer?' Amy cried.

Amy's mother gave her a hug. 'God always answers prayers,' she smiled. 'Sometimes he says "yes", sometimes "no" and sometimes "wait". This time God said "no".'

'But why?' Amy asked puzzled.

'I don't know Amy,' her mother replied, 'but maybe one day you will.'

'Why hasn't God answered
my prayer?' Amy cried.

Some time later Amy went on an adventure to India. She wanted to tell the people there about the love of Jesus. Very few people knew about the one true God. Some even sold their babies to temple priests. The priests did not look after these children, so Amy tried to rescue as many as she could. Often in the middle of the night she would run off on really big adventures, to rescue babies and bring them home to live with her.

Amy went on an adventure to India.
She wanted to tell the people there
about the love of Jesus.

One night Amy crept up to the temple door and listened. A baby was crying. Quickly Amy ran, picked up the baby, and cuddled her. The baby looked up at Amy's soft brown eyes and smiled. Amy smiled back.

'I know now why God gave me brown eyes,' Amy thought as she walked quickly home. 'Brown eyes are not scary for little Indian babies. Blue eyes would be too strange for them. When God said "No", he gave me just the right answer,' Amy said.

'When God said "No", he gave me
just the right answer,' Amy said.

For the kids at the Drakies club.
Give your life to Jesus when you're young.
He always listens to you.

© Copyright 2005 Catherine Mackenzie
Reprinted 2008 and 2011
ISBN:978-1-84550-108-2
Published by Christian Focus Publications,
Geanies House, Fearn, Tain, Ross-shire, IV20 1TW,
Scotland, U.K.
www.christianfocus.com
Illustrated by Rita Ammassari
Cover design by Daniel van Straaten
Printed in China
Other titles in this series:
Corrie ten Boom: Are all the watches safe? 978-1-84550-109-9
John Calvin: What is the truth? 978-1-84550-560-8
David Livingstone: Who is the bravest? 978-1-84550-384-0
Martin Luther: What should I do? 978-1-84550-561-5
George Müller: Does money grow on trees? 978-1-84550-110-5
Helen Roseveare: What's in the parcel? 978-1-84550-383-3
Hudson Taylor: Could somebody pass the salt? 978-1-84550-111-2